The Really Short Poems
of A. R. Ammons

BY A. R. AMMONS

Ommateum
Expressions of Sea Level
Corsons Inlet
Tape for the Turn of the Year
Northfield Poems
Selected Poems
Uplands
Briefings
Collected Poems: 1951–1971
(winner of the National Book Award for Poetry, 1973)
Sphere: The Form of a Motion
(winner of the 1973–1974 Bollingen Prize in Poetry)
Diversifications
The Snow Poems
Highgate Road
The Selected Poems: 1951–1977
Selected Longer Poems
A Coast of Trees
*(winner of the National Book Critics Circle
Award for Poetry, 1981)*
Worldly Hopes
Lake Effect Country
The Selected Poems: Expanded Edition

The
Really
Short
Poems of
A. R. Ammons

W· W· NORTON & COMPANY

New York · London

The text of this book is composed in Aster, with display
type set in Raleigh Medium. Composition and manufac-
turing by the Maple-Vail Book Manufacturing Group.
Book design by Charlotte Staub.
First Edition

Library of Congress Cataloging-in-Publication Data

Ammons, A. R., 1926–
    The really short poems of A. R. Ammons.
        p. cm.
    I. Title.
PS3501.M6R4   1990
811'.54—dc20   89-71357

ISBN 0-393-02870-4

W. W. Norton & Company, Inc.
500 Fifth Avenue, New York, N.Y. 10110
W. W. Norton & Company, Ltd.
10 Coptic Street, London WC1A 1PU

1 2 3 4 5 6 7 8 9 0

ACKNOWLEDGMENTS

About thirty of these pieces are taken from my *Collected Poems 1951–71*, no longer in print, and other poems are from subsequent volumes, all published by Norton.

About twenty of the poems come from *Highgate Road*, a privately printed, limited edition of thirty-six copies, 1977.

The poems "Market Adviser" and "Stills" first appeared in *Words on the Page, The World in Your Hands*, Book 1, edited by Lipkin and Solotaroff, Harper & Row, New York, 1990.

Many of the poems first appeared in *Pembroke Magazine* number 18, edited by Shelby Stephenson, Pembroke, North Carolina.

"For Doyle Fosso" was a limited edition by Press for Privacy; "Whitelash of Air Rapids" first appeared in *Epoch;* "Capture" in the *Grapevine;* "Ah" in *The Hudson Review;* "Cracking a Few Hundred Million Years" in *Manhattan Review;* "Late Look" in *Mississippi Review;* "Spring Tornado" in *New Letters*. My thanks to the editors.

And my warm appreciation to Elizabeth Davey for invaluable help with the manuscript, summer 1989.

CONTENTS

Weathering   *1*

Release   *2*

After Yesterday   *3*

Recovery   *4*

Hype   *5*

Increment   *6*

Sitting Down, Looking Up   *7*

Mirrorment   *8*

Over and Done With   *9*

Attention   *10*

Double Exposure   *11*

Turning   *12*

Weight   *13*

Cousins   *14*

Trigger   *15*

Reflective   *16*

Equilibrations   *17*

Second Party   *18*

Digging Wonder   *19*

Tryst   *20*

Success Story   *21*

Glacials   *22*

Stoning Stone   23

Triplet   *24*

Substantial Planes   *25*

North Street   *26*

Spaceship   *27*

Settlement   *28*

Spruce Woods   *29*

Self   *30*

I Went Back   *31*

Deaf Zone   *32*

Coming To   *33*

Natives   *34*

Precious Weak Fields   *35*

Scarecrow   *36*

Lofty   *37*

Immediacy   *38*

Filling in the Dots   *39*

Figuring Belief   *40*

Wiring   *41*

Crinkling Trails   *42*

Transducer   *43*

Sizing   *44*

Bride   *45*

Cracking a Few Hundred
   Million Years   *46*

Oblivion's Bloom   *47*

Soul's Seas   *48*

Correction   *49*

Clarifications   *50*

Celestial Dealings   *51*

Waking   *52*

Glass Specialty   *53*

Small Song   *54*

Pedagogy Agog   *55*

Touching   *56*

Planet Actions   *57*

Holding On   *58*

Worky Shallows   *59*

Hollows   *60*

Still Frame   *61*

Timing   *62*

This   *63*

Spring Tornado   *64*

Bottommost   *65*

Time Spans   *66*

Crow Ride   *67*

Roundel   *68*

Calling   *69*

That Day   *70*

Poetry to the Rescue   *71*

Soaker   *72*

Miss   *73*

Merchandise   *74*

Ah   *75*

Transfer   *76*

Fortitude   *77*

Pebble's Story   *78*

Providence   *79*

Whitelash of Air Rapids   *80*

Meeting the Opposition   *81*

Late November   *82*

Photosynthesis   *83*

Leaning Up   *84*

Winter Sanctuaries *85*

Anxiety *86*

Twangs & Little Twists *87*

Winter Scene *88*

Bay Bank *89*

Night Post *90*

Late Look *91*

Mediation *92*

Grove's Way *93*

Nearing Equinox *94*

Circling Splinters *95*

Squall Ball *96*

Rainy Morning *97*

Teleology *98*

Negligence These Days *99*

Down Low *100*

Exotic *101*

Chasm *102*

Theory Center *103*

Around Here *104*

Progress Report *105*

Catch *106*

Night Chill   *107*
Salute   *108*
Shading Flight In   *109*
Snow Roost   *110*
Glass Globe   *111*
For Doyle Fosso   *112*
The Scour   *113*
Grisly Grit   *114*
Reading   *115*
One Thing and Another   *116*
Enough   *117*
Close Relations   *118*
Recording   *119*
Spring Clearing   *120*
Resurrections   *121*
Poem   *122*
Juice   *123*
Camels   *124*
Course Work   *125*
Gardening   *126*
Quit That   *127*
Swoggled   *128*

Likely Story   *129*

Market Adviser   *130*

Stills   *131*

Bulletin   *132*

The Upshot   *133*

Milepost   *134*

Coming Right Up   *135*

Their Sex Life   *136*

Kingpin   *137*

Cleavage   *138*

Kith   *139*

Imaginary Number   *140*

Layabout   *141*

Resolve   *142*

Cold Rheum   *143*

The Mark   *144*

Immoderation   *145*

Blue Skies   *146*

Utensil   *147*

Reorganization   *148*

Preexistence   *149*

Undersea   *150*

Permanence   *151*
Songlet   *152*
Coward   *153*
Interference   *154*
Orchard   *155*
Lost and Found   *156*
Communication   *157*
Modality   *158*
Capture   *159*
For Louise and Tom Gossett   *160*

The Really Short Poems
of A. R. Ammons

WEATHERING

A day without rain is like
a day without sunshine

RELEASE

After a long
muggy
hanging
day
the raindrops
started so
sparse
the bumblebee flew
between
them home.

AFTER
YESTERDAY

After yesterday
afternoon's blue
clouds and white rain
the mockingbird
in the backyard
untied the drops from
leaves and twigs
with a long singing.

RECOVERY

All afternoon
the tree shadows, accelerating,
lengthened
till
sunset
shot them black into infinity:
next morning
darkness
returned from the other
infinity and the
shadows caught ground
and through the morning, slowing,
hardened into noon.

HYPE

A pollen
fly makes

so much
of sounding

like a
bee because

he has
no sting.

INCREMENT

Applause is a shower
to the watertable of
self-regard:
in the downpour
the watertable's irrelevant
but after the shower passes
possibility takes on
an extensive millimeter.

SITTING DOWN,
LOOKING UP

A silver jet,
riding the top of tundra clouds,
comes over
maybe from Rio:
the aluminum sun shines
on it
as if it were a natural creature.

MIRRORMENT

Birds are flowers flying
and flowers perched birds.

OVER AND
DONE WITH

Continually is continuously
from time to time

and continuously is
continually all the time.

ATTENTION

Down by the bay I
kept in mind
at once
the tips of all the rushleaves
and so
came to know
balance's cost and true:
somewhere though in the whole field
is the one
tip
I will someday lose out of mind
and fall through.

DOUBLE
EXPOSURE

Flounderlike, poetry
flattens white
against bottom mud

so farthest tremors can get
full-ranged to the bone:
but on the side if flowers

invisible with blue mud-work
imitations, it
turns both eyes.

TURNING

From reality's flowing flurry
take out a glass bead
and steer round &
round
it, an everlasting:
the center's in there,
its invisibility seen through.

WEIGHT

He loved cloud covers,
went into woods
to hide from stars: he
wept under bridges,
noticed weeds, counted
frog calls
till a stone in
his belly hardened
against infinity, the
grievances of levitation.

COUSINS

Hornets nesting under the weatherboarding
drop by the window: I think them

catkins the wind's picked from the birch nearby
then notice they drop

funneling centrally from expanse:
mind alters agreeably to convergences home.

TRIGGER

I almost step on
a huge spider:
it stalls and
disperses
like oil-beads on water,
baby spiders
shedding radially
till a skinny
mother hardly
shades the
spent center.

REFLECTIVE

I found a
weed
that had a

mirror in it
and that
mirror

looked in at
a mirror
in

me that
had a
weed in it

EQUILIBRATIONS

If you walk back
and forth

through a puddle pretty
soon

you wet the whole
driveway but of

course dry
the puddle up.

SECOND
PARTY

I learn from the lake,
whole, composed,
whose shores thrash

wind-songs, that
I might trouble
you with an edge of

praise: I
stand by you
as complete as

you have made me
and praise will allow.

DIGGING
WONDER

Immediacy's stone
has

outlasted

every other
stone

TRYST

I'm to go see you tonight:
birds that know where to fly
are loose under my ribs:

your eyes fly here to my mind's
eye: I dwell in them:
what if I'm frozen

when I see you; what if I burn
completely up: the birds
may break out and go

too soon; or, too bad
if my self flies to you
early, and I can't follow.

SUCCESS STORY

h

I never got on good
relations with the world

first I had nothing
the world wanted

then the world had
nothing I wanted

GLACIALS

In the geological rock garden
split boulders
lie about as kinds and ages,

a hundred million years or more in
many frozen solid:
dusty thaws flow

steam-loose from the surfaces and
wind on the way
at last, the wind mixing

old and current time
in mixings beginning and
ended, time unbegun, unended.

STONING
STONE

I put down
the splintered ax

and in the
fury of failure

attacked time's
stone with

tears: the stone
holds, but tears

soften the stone
of my striving.

TRIPLET

Iris leaves
threes-in-one
cut
broadside into sun and rain
to send high
flop loose the
hairy huzzy
iris bloom

SUBSTANTIAL
PLANES

It doesn't
matter

to me
if

poems mean
nothing:

there's no
floor

to the
universe

and yet
one

walks the
floor.

NORTH STREET

I tipped my head
to go under the
low boughs but

the sycamore mistook
my meaning and
bowed back.

SPACESHIP

It's amazing all
this motion going
on and
water can lie still
in glasses and the gas
can in the
garage doesn't rattle.

SETTLEMENT

It snowed
last night

and this
morning no

track in or

out shows
on the

cemetery
road.

SPRUCE WOODS

It's so still
today that a
dipping bough means
a squirrel
has gone through.

SELF

I wake up from
a nap
and sense a
well in myself:
I have
dropped into
the well:
the ripples
have just
vanished

I WENT BACK

I went back
to my old home
and the furrow
of each year
plowed like
surf across
the place had
not washed
memory away.

DEAF ZONE

Last night's
drizzle's
this morning's

rushed
brook:
the ledge roars

so,
look both ways
crossing the road,

the
brook's passing
louder than cars'.

COMING TO

Like a steel drum
cast at sea
my days,
banged and dented
by a found shore of
ineradicable realities,
sandsunk, finally, gaping,
rustsunk in
compass grass

NATIVES

Logos is an engine
myth fuels,
civilization
a pattern,
scalelike crust
on a hill
but the hill's swell
derives from
gravity's
deep fluids
centering elsewhere
otherwise

PRECIOUS WEAK FIELDS

Mercy's so slight it's like
a glitter-bit in granite or a single
pane-sun in snow flint or the warp-weave of
slice-light netting a shallows stone.

SCARECROW

Nature's undoings
let
the maple rise

close in on the young dead elm,
the new
branches paralleling

trails along
the old so
that the young elm

stands dry, held
upright in broad
becoming's long going.

LOFTY

No use to make any more
angels for the air,
the medium and residence of such:
gas is no state
to differentiate:
come down here to
bird and weed, stump
and addled fear and swirl up
unity's angelic spire,
rot lit in rising fire.

IMMEDIACY

On the way to
the eternal sea,
I looked for coins

in the gutter:
looked at the sea,
a deep summary;

returned along
the gutter
looking for coins.

FILLING IN
THE DOTS

Pigeons, thirty-five in a
speed, break

over the lombardies
just so

as, missing, to
outline the row.

FIGURING
BELIEF

Praying answers prayer:
in the deep spells
of inquiry and hope,
a self
enabled to rise again
to the compromises
and the shattering caring
forms

WIRING

Radiance comes from
on high and, staying,
sends down silk
lines to the flopping
marionette, me, but
love comes from
under the ruins and
sends the lumber up
limber into leaf that
touches so high it nearly
puts out the radiance

CRINKLING TRAILS

Snow's our winter brightening,
the sun far away and low
and, anyway, held away by clouds

the color of everything else:
but at night blank fields
disclose the tiniest traveler,

the source of light too diffuse
to find or hide from or to
hide any side of a thing or

action, mouse rumpled in a fluff
of wings, black roses, leaf radials flung
up from undersnow by
daylight's digging crows.

TRANSDUCER

Solar floes
big as continents
plunge rasping
against each other:
the noise
flaring into space,
into thinner & thinner
material means,
becomes two million
degrees of heat.

SIZING

Some ideas hit
brush too thick
to mingle through
or clearings
too wide to bound

BRIDE

for Minfong Ho

Sometimes a maple seed
can hold on so
tight it spins
way out on the wind strong
enough to snap it free!

CRACKING A FEW HUNDRED
MILLION YEARS

So the plastic conduits for the new
phone system could be put down,

the big-clawed, wheeling
forehoe dug a trench

into the original shale-lyings,
soil mixing trench-side with broken stone:

this morning, after last night's
downpour, the ground smells

sour, a scent no human form was here to
know when the shale went down.

OBLIVION'S BLOOM

Struck head to
ground in
first cold
the bumblebee
turns
in the sweetest
nectar yet

SOUL'S SEAS

Tears for the long-gone times
and for the little time left to go

are the buoyancy whereby
the butterfly ship   -

gets wings to the wind and
flies, all energies exhilarations.

CORRECTION

The burdens of the world
on my back
lighten the world
not a whit while
removing them greatly
decreases my specific
gravity

CLARIFICATIONS

The crows, mingled
powder white,

arrive floundering
through the

heavy snowfall:
they land ruffling

stark black
on the spruce boughs and

chisel the neighborhood
sharp with their cries.

CELESTIAL
DEALINGS

The heaped hemlock
boughs hardly
sway in the
profound cold,
snow, anyway,
too quick to miss.

WAKING

The oak grove's
a lake on
stilts:

underwater boulder-boughs
define
standing clarities:

in gusts waves
nod,
plunge toward breaking.

GLASS SPECIALTY

The redbird, nesting
in the nearby
yewbush, has found

a fluttering rival in
the garage window: pecking
as at a nectar of hatred,

he (not a hummingbird)
thrashingly sustains
himself before his image:

weakened to the ground, he
comes back up, the ruffling
rival there every time.

SMALL
SONG

The reeds give
way to the

wind and give
the wind away

PEDAGOGY
AGOG

The smart gain
knowledge

and learn to
express

themselves to join
the

world of power
where

it pays to
know

little and say
less.

TOUCHING

The spangled, mauve
hydrangea heads, having

nodded over upsidedown
with summer weight

and summer storms
now have their

bottoms topped
by fluffy cones of snow

heavy enough
to make them

going down
go on down.

PLANET ACTIONS

The spider, dashing from
marginal boughshade
to cross the driveway

hits the hot macadam
and, legs dancing,
scoots back for

the cool: brother,
I effuse, hot
weather we're having!

HOLDING ON

The stone in my tread
sings by the strip of woods
but is
unheard by open fields:

surround me then with walls
before I risk
the outer sight, as, walled,
I'll soon long to.

WORKY
SHALLOWS

The sun's angle's so
the creek's slow's
dim, flat, clear

but down where a shoal
breaks the flow thin and
fast—shattered into curves

and runlets—
the sun blinds everything
white with action.

HOLLOWS

The whirlwind lifts
sand into itself to hide

holy spun emptiness or to
erect a tall announcement

where formed
emptiness is to be found.

STILL FRAME

The wind played
down frost-still,

sunrise brings three
crows
into the nearly

empty sugar
maple, their

pitching and flapping
jarring a touch of gold leaves loose
that

sprinkles down as if
picked by a breeze.

TIMING

The year's run out
to the tip
blossom on the snapdragon
stalk.

THIS

time will wash
away

so

clean not a
cry

will

be left in
it

SPRING
TORNADO

Trees lash, warp:
the low-down
drops over the ridge

valley-deep through here:
terror pops out
like shoots or buds,

just the sky to be
left whole.

BOTTOMMOST

We circle the sinkhole
the coil spins in:
when the speed is close and sufficient,
a tube of nothingness
opens down which
attracted objects mill exodus.

TIME
SPANS

What lightning
strikes

in an
instant the

boulder hums
all year

CROW RIDE

When the crow
lands, the
tip of the sprung spruce

bough weighs
so low, the
system so friction-free,

the bobbing lasts
way past any
interest in the subject.

ROUNDEL

When unity, having found its way throughout,
draws all things into a
single bloat, manyness slices

the innermost layer and pushes the skin away
and there as before in all its profusion and
differentiation is the world again, hail, sleet,
    mist-ice, snow

CALLING

Wind rocks
the porch chairs

somebody home

THAT DAY

You came to see me one day and
as usual in such matters

things grew significant—
what you believed, the way you

turned or leaned: when
you left, our area tilted, a

tile, and whatever
opposes desolation slid away.

POETRY
TO THE RESCUE

You must be
nearly lost to
be (if
found) nearly
found

SOAKER

You can appreciate
this kind of rain,
thunderless,
small-gauged
after a dry spell,
the wind quiet,
multitudes of leaves
as if yelling
the smallest thanks.

MISS

Wonder if
you're gross
consider the cosmic
particle so scant
it can splink all
the way through
Cheops
nicking nothing

MERCHANDISE

When we have
played with
the toy life

death takes it
back without
condition

whatever the condition

AH

When the forehead drains
and the limbs akimbo
freeze

so that the body can
be carried as
by stubs a log

the true sigh is not
yet but when
ground-packed

the tendons slip the
joints, the muscles run,
the bones chink loose.

TRANSFER

When the bee lands the
morning glory bloom
dips some and weaves:
   the coming true of
   weight
   from weightless wing-held
   air
   seems at the touch
   implausible.

FORTITUDE

We should think
we can get
by with a
setback or two:

the lawn makes
a life of
starting over and
swirly bugs

in dusk air,
prey, get where
they're going
changing course.

PEBBLE'S STORY

Wearing away
wears

wearing
away away

PROVIDENCE

To stay
bright as
if just
thought of
earth requires
only that
nothing stay

WHITELASH OF
AIR RAPIDS

This bright morning, the
leaves hardly dipping,

it's okay to be out
under trees, the elms

and sugar maples deadwood
cleared by yesterday's sucking

thundergusts when the leaves
turned on, lifting,

the high branches and maple
and elm logs

floated plunging in
the lofts on sleeves and roils of air.

MEETING THE OPPOSITION

The wind sidles up to
and brusquely in a swell flattens
lofting one side
of the spirea bush:
but the leaves have

so many edges, angles
and varying curvatures that
the wind on the other side
seeps out in a
gentle management.

LATE
NOVEMBER

The white sun
like a moth
on a string
circles the southpole.

PHOTOSYNTHESIS

The sun's wind
blows the fire
green, sails the
chloroplasts,
lifts banks, bogs,
boughs into flame:
the green ash of
yellow loss.

LEANING UP

The storm that downed
the living pine
left the dead hickory

standing:
barkless, stub-knobbed,
den-hole riddled,

the hickory
will
be around while

the heavy, heaving living
carry on carrying
nearly too much to bear alive.

WINTER SANCTUARIES

The squirrel, bunching branches,
knits a billowing raft
from twig-ends and, riding air, lifts
one paw to pull in a tip
where maple seeds, shaken, cling.

ANXIETY

The sparrowhawk
flies hard to

stand in the
air: something

about direction
lets us loose

into ease
and slow grace.

TWANGS &
LITTLE TWISTS

The snow polished
hard after
day-melt,

the squirrel's
scratchy paws on
strict

ice sound like
my shoes'
scritchy squish.

WINTER SCENE

There is now not a single
leaf on the cherry tree:

except when the jay
plummets in, lights, and,

in pure clarity, squalls:
then every branch

quivers and
breaks out in blue leaves.

BAY BANK

The redwing blackbird
lighting
dips deep the
windy bayridge
reed but
sends a song up
reed and wind rise to.

NIGHT POST

The philodendron's ear-leaf
by the

window
listens for the moon.

LATE LOOK

The last one
died and she
shook with relief,

her house free
from the threat of
sick old people

only to see in
the mirror an
old woman arriving.

MEDIATION

The grove kept us dry,
subtracting from
the shower much
immediacy:

but then distracted us
for hours, dropping
snaps faint as the twigs
of someone coming.

GROVE'S WAY

The campus oakgrove is
something (specially now

with the elms gone)
the branchlofts subsuming vast

congregations,
the trunks centuries through—

but a guy wire's been run
to hold in one

tree on the edge being
leaned out of the grove.

NEARING EQUINOX

The boundaries, fought clear, are abandoned,
now, and the robins fly in bunches over
common ground: drift, return in near reversals,

but, on the whole, feed south—yew berries
reddening, the honeysuckle berries dried up,
crickets, fall fat, singing all night.

CIRCLING SPLINTERS

Summer's coming's summer's going:
only leaving brings returning:

things rise, stand, drown:
winter shows summer's sticks

and no summer comes
again when summer comes.

SQUALL BALL

Squalls rounder
than the sky exclude
the sun

till brightness
like a loose thread
showing on the

west ridge unravels
hedgerows
and fields into light.

RAINY MORNING

Sometimes the ridge across
the way transluminous
emerges above the mist
and squares and detached rondures
of vapory ground with
dairy barns and old trees
break out afloat
separated in high lyings

TELEOLOGY

Some things
are so

big that
it's hard

to tell
you're going

round going
round them.

NEGLIGENCE
THESE DAYS

Somebody left a ladder
flat

on the university
grounds

so the mower
couldn't

get over it and
grass

and weeds filled
its

intervals with spindly
ascendancy.

DOWN LOW

Snowstorms high-traveling,
furry clouds blur over
our zero air:
wind steams (or
smokes) fine snow
off the eaves, settled ghosts
trailing up and away:
the pheasant, too cold to
peck, stands on one foot
like a stiff weed.

EXOTIC

Science outstrips
other modes &
reveals more of
the crux of the matter
than we can calmly
handle

CHASM

Put	your
self	out
and	you're
not	quite
up	to
it	or
all	in

THEORY
CENTER

Poetry if
not the

criticism of
life is

the life
of criticism

AROUND HERE

Our trees seem leaflesser
than anybody's in January:

ice scum-wrinkles ponds
in arctic flashes:

our clouds bollix sunny
forty-six ways:

our falls, dumb
columns at

fifteen below, purport
perpetual motion.

PROGRESS REPORT

Now I'm
into things

so small
when I

say boo
I disappear

CATCH

Near dusk: approaching
my house, I see
over the roof

the quartermoon
and, aiming, walk it
down my chimney flue.

NIGHT CHILL

My big round yew
can stand a gust
into a million
presences: too
many needles
to get through
to get through
except drift through:
birds in there peep and sleep,
puffy in the slow hurry.

SALUTE

May happiness
pursue you,

catch you
often, and,

should it
lose you,

be waiting
ahead, making

a clearing
for you.

SHADING FLIGHT IN

Lit clouds diffuse tree
shadows etiolated long
across the grass-gold winter
lawn, trunks and branches as if
risen aground to a deep
remembrance:
substances—there may not always
be wood, but insubstantial shadow
will always find a solid source.

SNOW ROOST

Last night the
fluffiest inhabitant

filled the
cedar forks deep, but this

windy morning,
gusts blizzard-sharp

explode clumps of flight
into local blindings.

GLASS GLOBE

I woke up (merely) and found
myself
inside a bulb of pain:
I said
everybody else looks all right,
it must be mine:
I kept it & kept it
shined invisibly clear.

FOR DOYLE FOSSO

I walked at night and
became alarmed
at the high lights and amplitude
but passed a brook
the sound of whose
breaking water
took my whole attention.

THE SCOUR

It was so windy
last night the snow
got down nowhere
except up against something.

GRISLY GRIT

It's so cold
the snow doesn't

need clouds to
snow from: it

fines right out
of the air,

humidity's immediate sift,
and, nearly weightless,

settles as if against
its will all over.

READING

It's nice
after dinner
to walk down to
the beach

and find
the biggest
thing on earth
relatively calm.

ONE THING
AND ANOTHER

It is one
thing

to know one
thing

and another
thing

to know another
thing.

ENOUGH

I thought the
woods afire
or some
house behind the
trees
but it was
the wind
sprung loose
by a random
thunderstorm
smoking pollen fog
from the
evergreens

CLOSE RELATIONS

Islands dry out enlarging
on the
brook's slate bottom

while the sky-shallows
of lessening
pools

shimmy
to
the feathery trickle.

RECORDING

I remember when freezing
rain bent the yearling
pine over and stuck its
crown to ground ice:
but now it's spring
and the pine stands
up straight, frisky in
the breeze, except for
memory, a little lean.

SPRING CLEARING

I pull dead shafts
out of the spirea clump but
some branched rootknots,
split off,
hook stuck:
I let them go another year:
decay will loosen them.

RESURRECTIONS

In spring
a bluster
busting up

against a
wall will
lift last

year's leaves
higher than
trees did.

POEM

In a high wind the
leaves don't
fall but fly
straight out of the
tree like birds

JUICE

I'm stuck with the infinity thing
again this morning: a skinny
inexpressible syrup, finer than light,
everywhere present: the cobweb becoming
visible with dust and the tumblelint
stalled in the corner seem worthy.

CAMELS

I like nonliterary,
uneducated people,
beach riffraff:
they are so aloof and
unengageable: you
can rope them with
no interest of your own.

COURSE
WORK

Ideas go
through most
heads without

picking up

any substance
or leaving
any trace

GARDENING

I'd give bushels of blooms
to bank my hardy cover
into your cushion mums

QUIT THAT

I don't
want to

be taken
seriously except

that I
want my

wish not
to be

taken seriously
to be

taken seriously

SWOGGLED

I'd rather
be
suckled by
an
outworn pagan
than
get my
horn
wreathed in
an
old triton.

LIKELY
STORY

I'd up
up up

if there
were any

up to
up up.

MARKET
ADVISER

If you're
not in

it for
the ups

and downs
you might

as well
get out

of it
she said

STILLS

I have nowhere
to go and

nowhere to go

when I get
back from there

BULLETIN

I mentioned trimming
the bushes and
the squirrels cleared
their nuts out of there

THE
UPSHOT

It's hard
to live

living it
up down.

MILEPOST

I've been married
forty years and
in all that
time I haven't
been unfaithful once:
lately, I haven't
even been faithful.

COMING
RIGHT UP

One can't
have it

both ways
and both

ways is
the only

way I
want it.

THEIR
SEX LIFE

One failure on
Top of another

KINGPIN

One fellow turns all
ladies into ladies
of waiting till
he would be served
but when he would
be served he is (alas)
oft kept awaiting.

CLEAVAGE

Soon	as
you	stop
having	trouble
getting	down
to	earth
you	start
having	trouble
getting	off
the	ground

KITH

The *de*
on one

end of
decide doesn't

look like
the *de*

on the
other end

IMAGINARY NUMBER

The difference between
me &

nothing is
zero.

LAYABOUT

The early
bird catches

the worm
but I'd

just as
soon be

late and
catch hell.

RESOLVE

We must work
in the spirit
of unity and
cooperation; I'll supply
the unity and
you supply the
cooperation.

COLD
RHEUM

You can't
tell what's

snot from
what's not

THE
MARK

I hope I'm
not right
where frost
strikes the
butterfly:
in the back
between
the wings.

IMMODERATION

If something is too
big, enlarging it
may correct it:

a skinny thing
acquires great force
pushed next to nothing.

BLUE
SKIES

If I leaped
I would
plunge over the
pinetops into
the deepest sea

UTENSIL

How does the pot pray:
wash me, so I gleam?

prays, crack my enamel:
let the rust in.

REORGANIZATION

High wind yesterday
snapped the top
off the big
pine by the
golf course, leaving
a single bough,
once lowest, highest.

PREEXISTENCE

Guided by
none the

snowflakes draw
crowfeet white

in the
spruce boughs.

UNDERSEA

Foraminiferal millennia
bank and spill but
even so
time's under pressure of
diatomaceous event,
divisions a moment
arcs across:
              desperate
for an umbrella, net, longpole,
or fan: so much
to keep for paradigm,
so much to lose.

PERMANENCE

Eyes shined
for life

by a
bright loss.

SONGLET

Death, unduly undoing,
kisses us awake into
the new world and leaves

us preempted and unsteady:
oh, here we go, we say,
another adjustment as usual:

light appears to be the leader
here: we turn to where
a beam forms and set out

COWARD

Bravery runs in my family.

INTERFERENCE

A whirlwind in the fields
lifts sand
into its motions
to show, tight, small,
the way it walks
through a summer day:

better take time to watch
the sand-shadow mist—
since every
grain of sand
is being counted by the sun.

ORCHARD

Art's the
fruit of

the trees
of pain

that grow
in the

fields of
unspent life.

LOST AND FOUND

Apostasy is such, if you doubt on,
You return by the road you set out on.

COMMUNICATION

All day—I'm
surprised—the
orange tree, windy, sunny,
has said nothing:
nevertheless,
four ripe oranges have
dropped and several
dozen
given up a ghost of green.

MODALITY

A grackle
flicks
down from
the cedar
onto
the shiny
alley
to see
if the
shower softened
the garbage
bags.

CAPTURE

After the long snow,
the sun strikes a winded-free
side of the car:

the air twenty, metal, though,
takes up heat and
melt trickling down

freezes like mangrove
roots,
grounding the car still.

FOR LOUISE AND TOM GOSSETT

After a creek
drink
the goldfinch
lights in

the bank willow
which
drops the brook
a yellow leaf.